T0380909

TO DAD

POLISH OFFICER MURDERED IN KATYŃ

Poems

with Historical Essays

by

WITOMIŁA WOŁK-JEZIERSKA

Daughter of Lieutenant Wincenty Wołk

Libra Institute, Inc.

2019

Poems: Witomiła Wołk-Jezierska
Translation of Poems: Wojciech Graniczewski and M. B. Szonert
Editor: M. B. Szonert
Cover Photo: Libra Institute, Inc.

ISBN: Softcover   978-1-7960-2018-2
         EBook   978-1-7960-2017-5

Print information available on the last page

Rev. date: 03/14/2019

To order additional copies of this book, contact:
Xlibris
1-888-795-4274
www.Xlibris.com
Orders@Xlibris.com

or

Libra Institute, Inc.
Akron, Ohio, USA
www.librainstitute.org
librainstitute74@gmail.com

TABLE OF CONTENTS

ABOUT THE AUTHOR 4

FOREWORD 5

TO DAD 7

TO PARENTS 9

A POSTCARD FROM KOZIELSK 11

THE DEAD FOREST 13

TURN BACK THE CLOCK! 15

FATHER, DAD 17

THE MEMORY OF TIME 19

DAD'S MILITARY SHIRT 21

DREAM ABOUT THE FATHER 23

MEMORY 25

MY MOTHER - KATYŃ PENELOPE......................................27

APRIL FIFTH 1989 29

A HANDFUL OF SOIL 31

MY FATHER:
A PORTRAIT FROM IMAGINATION 32

THE FAMILY DEFINED BY KATYŃ 37

KATYŃ EXECUTION ORDER
MARCH 5, 1940, USSR POLITBIURO 45

USSR POLITBIURO ON DEPORTATIONS
MARCH 2, 1940 47

SHELAPIN'S MEMO..49

MADDEN COMMITTEE
FINAL REPORT, DECEMBER 22, 1952 51

LIST OF PHOTOGRAPHS 52

ABOUT THE AUTHOR

Witomiła Wołk-Jezierska was born on January 22, 1940. At the time of her birth, her father, officer of the Polish Army Wincenty Wołk, was held by the Soviets in the Kozielsk prisoner-of-war camp. On April 30, 1940, Wincenty Wołk was brutally murdered by the NKVD in the Katyń forest near Smolensk. Witomiła never saw her father, but her entire adult life she has been on the forefront of the fight for truth, justice and atonement for the crime of all crimes - the Katyń genocide - thus far in vain...

The poems *"To Dad"* have been inspired by the trauma of one of the most horrific crimes in the human history aggravated by repercussions that followed such as the perpetuation of the Katyń lie, international cover-up, impunity of the perpetrators, inability to recover the remains of the victims, ruthless persecution and coercion of the families, massive censorship, disinformation, and above all, the conspiracy of silence that lasted for generations. The poems sharpen our perception of the intensity and uniqueness of depth and length of agony experienced by the Katyń families. They give testimony to unbearable adversity of several generations of the Polish people deeply harmed and wounded by the Soviet Union, abandoned, marginalized, and ignored by the entire world for decades. The poems are supplemented by historical essays, which put the eradication of the Polish elites in Katyń in the historical context.

From among the family of Witomiła's father, on April 13, 1940, NKVD deported his mother and sister along with four young children to Kazakhstan. From among the family of Witomiła's mother, NKVD deported eight underage children and nine adults to the Arctic Circle.

Witomiła's other cousins who served in the Polish Army were also murdered by the Soviets:

- Capt. Kazimierz Burnatowicz, who was murdered in Kharkov and buried in Piatykhatky;
- Capt. Franciszek Głowacz, murdered in a location undisclosed for 80 years;
- Sec. Lt. Antoni Szancer, murdered in a location undisclosed for 80 years;
- A Major of the Border Defense Corps Jan Wojciechowski murdered on the way to Kołyma;
- Lt. Szczęsny-Brończyk, murdered in Kołyma.

Witomiła has written extensively on Katyń. Her works include a volume of poetry entitled *You Come When I Think of Katyń*, award-winning books, for example *Our Father in the Pits*, and articles *A Portrait from Memory*. As an artist specializing in graphic design and art conservation, she served as Chief Graphic Designer for the National Theater in Warsaw, and contributed to the preservation of treasurable manuscripts such as works by F. Chopin. She was recognized by the Polish Ministry of Culture with Cultural Activist Award and Golden Badge for Preservation of Historic Monuments. She is also a recipient of Pro Memoria and Pro Patria medals.

FOREWORD

My entire life is one big battle over my art. I have the right to create the way I think; the way I feel. In order to create the convincing art, the artist has to show his inner self, who he is, where he comes from, and where he goes.

The scream… scream of life… to tell you who I am and how I feel. The liberty and truth are indispensable to creation. Who are we with no liberty to tell the truth? - The captives…

ANDRZEJ PITYŃSKI
Sculptor
Katyń Monument, Jersey City

Photo No. 3.

Photo No. 4. Winceny Wołk, Polish Army Officer imprisoned in Kozielsk - murdered in Katyń.

TO DAD

I call you
through distance
through time,
into the forest
into the Katyń Grave,
I whisper
that dearest name
with tears,
with the pulse of my blood
I accuse…

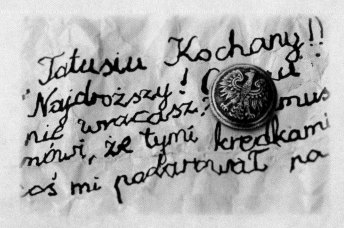

Arise,
follow my voice,
come and leave
a trace –
rain like tears,
flame like
love;
embrace me with wind.

Revive
in pine tree bark
in candlelike flowers
in hairlike needles
in the sod soft as skin
remind us
that - you were …

As flaxen smoke
fly away
into space.

Translation: WG

Photo no. 6: Winceny Wołk and Ojcumiła Gancarz Wołk, Parents of the Author.

TO PARENTS

... scorching platform
your green uniform
her flowery dress
and your eyes, lips and hands
full of love
   -   this is farewell.
Days...
Months
    time passes by
-   this is waiting.
And death?
Death is – dawn
    is – Kosogorsk forest
    in assassins' embracing grip
    shout
    and
       fear
    Nagan bang
    ... deadly sweat
    embrace of trees
    and whirl of escaping
       thoughts...
    In memory - a green uniform
    the warmth of your hands
       ... and ...this forest
       - in it is the longing.

Translation: MSB

Photo No. 7: April 10, 1940 Postcard from Wincenty Wołk in Kozielsk to Maria Gancarowa - Grandmother of the Author.

A POSTCARD FROM KOZIELSK

In Your card,
so small –
       is everything I have from You:
       the joy of remembrance
       the pain of apartness
       a faint bewilderment
       that I am
       a part of You and Your name.

On a yellowed post card
Russian kolkhoz women –
censor all your words:
       of love,
       suffering
       painful helplessness,
       the effort to say everything,
       to reach everyone.
In those words, so simple
It is You all over - Father.

Translation: WG

Photo No. 8.

THE DEAD FOREST

That dead forest …
  where the wind
  froze in terror,
the birds
  deafened by gunshots
and only the pine trees
  weep their needles onto
  the sod of the Ditches
this is KATYŃ
There - THEY - rest.

Translation: WG

Photo No. 9. Master Pityński at the Katyń Monument against the backdrop of WTC, 1991

Photo No. 10. The Katyń Monument in Jersey City, September 11, 2001.

TURN BACK THE CLOCK!

You are dead!
    It is death that shouted to me
    Your name
    and the number:
    two thousand five hundred sixty-four!
And I -
    Nevertheless
    turn back the time
    with one word -
D A D
and... you come
    when I think –
K A T Y Ń

Translation: MBS

Photo No. 11. Tied hands of the exhumed Katyń Officer. Photo 1943

FATHER, DAD

Father, Dad -
The words never pronounced,
with a dry gunshot detached
from a child's lips …
with a hot wave they return when –
      in the depth of the Katyń ditches
      in the piles of firmly pressed bodies
      amongst the thousands of the martyred
            - our Fathers.

In their tied up hands
    power still trembles.
In their crushed skulls
    Memory still burns.
On their lips –
    Our names.
Their brains – gave us wisdom,
    their hearts – love
    their hands – kindness.
Bones merged in the tomb of martyrdom
gave us the power of waiting for justice.

Translation: WG

Photo No. 12.

THE MEMORY OF TIME

You speak
      with the wind of the Katyń Forest
you greet
      with a pine needle,
      a caress of the sun
         from Kosogory.

I wait
      for the wind
      for the sun
         that will dry the salty grief
         on my face
such is our talk.

Sometimes –
      a breeze is a windstorm,
      pinecones are bullets of death,
the sun terrified with a memory
      turns away from the earth in disgust
         – it is the memory of time …

Translation: WG

Photos No. 13. Husar by A. Pityński, Polish Cemetery in Doylestown, Pennsylvania. Photo G. Tymiński.

DAD'S MILITARY SHIRT

Saved from conflagration
Not discarded with the baggage in Katyń
The only one
Forgotten in a drawer
The Military Shirt of the Father

………………………………………..

I press to my lips
The fabric of his shirt
The hand rubs
material

    white

    thin

    old, not musty

I soothe it.

This shirt enfolds me.
Buttons

    sewed on a tape

    obedient to hands

    as back then

Bosom with small darts

    preserved frosted white

    of this quality material

Cuff

    wide,

    folded up

Clasp

    with a tear of pearl uterus

    hanged

    over the wrist

Low stand-up collar

    embraces my neck

    with fatherly cuddle.

Translation: MBS

Photo No. 14. Farewell by M. Jeliński

DREAM ABOUT THE FATHER

In Hades
      like for Eurydyka
into spatial azure
      like after a bird
      unconquerable
into the steppe
and into murkiness of water
bottomless
      I would follow You
for heaviness of Your hand
on a golden head
broad smile
and a flight from Your arms
high above the earth
....
and there in the Katyń Forest
I laid a flower.

Translation: MBS

Photo No. 15.

My mother and father knew each other since 1934. They married in 1938. They had one year of marriage only. It was a happy year because there were several families of young officers in Zambrów, they all were good friends. This happy time ended abruptly.

My mother… I can't imagine what she went through as a young person. She was just twenty something, she was 23-year-old when my father was murdered. The only sign of this very deep trauma is the fact that although she was a very attractive lady, great looking, very elegant, she never married again. The moment I started to work towards justice for the Katyń victims, she participated in everything. All petitions, the entire correspondence was done jointly with my mother, corrections, comments, recollections, this is my collaboration with my mother.

In 1997 my mother filed a motion with the Military Prosecutor's Office of the Russian Federation requesting information about my father - Lieutenant of the Polish Army Winceny Wołk. She received a reply that my father was "a prisoner of war in Kozielsk. He was killed in the spring of 1940 in Katyń."

At 95 years of age, my mother was still waiting. She was waiting not only for justice to be served for the Katyń crime but also she was waiting for him, for his return, now only for the return of his remains. This would be this fulfillment, this fulfillment of her lifelong struggle, these decades of waiting for him and for some semblance of justice to the Katyń families. She did not live to see it happen… She passed away on January 10, 2014.

MEMORY

There is time
when memory still carries
    the aroma of hair
    touch of a hand, voice
still reverberate
steps throughout the rooms
The image remained
    full
    firm
with the color of your face
    eyes.
Once
in the capricious streak
    of memory
details will disappear
    of sensory experience
maybe - will remain the love
    of what it was
reverie of the time
    passed.
An unexpected photograph
you will hold in hand
lovingly press
    to your face
closing your eyes
recall what can yet
    be remembered.

Translation: MBS

Photos No. 16. Katyń Families at the unveiling of the Katyń Memorial, London, UK, 1976.

MY MOTHER - KATYŃ PENELOPE

To my Mother – Ojcumiła Wołk

Penelope –
You are love
     fidelity
     remembrance
So many young and handsome
     around you
So many interested in you
…
and you, Penelope, - weave endlessly
     green fabric
You wait
bleached by time
And the fabric
why? …. blushes
     like hawthorn
…
You are like Hekate
thrown on your lap – the Body
Dripping with blood
     which flows on folds of the dress
to coagulate on the ground
at your feet.
…
You are like an animal
     Howling for the loss

You are the heart
    heavy
    like a stone
the blind
blindly, unconsciously
believing in the endurance of love
when nothing diminishes, disappears
despite the distance
…
The conscience of the crime
you are
my Mother – Penelope.

Translation: MBS

Photo No. 17

APRIL FIFTH 1989

The cry rips out our viscera,
interweaves with a Mazurka.
The Cross of Katyń Golgotha
at a standstill, outstretches its arms,
in brightness unites
everlasting greenery of the trees,
whiteness of snow,
our despair.

… screech of wheels!
… howl of cars!
… shouts of killers!
… crash of shots!

The Cross calms
the ceaseless sob,
covers us
with white down of snow
as, once, Them.

Photo No. 18. Mass in Katyń, April 5, 1989

Translation: MBS

Photo No. 19. KATYŃ Monument by A. Pityński, Baltimore, Maryland, USA.

A HANDFUL OF SOIL

After infinitude of waiting
I have You here with me
in a handful of soil,
in a needle of pine,
unexpected grass – you appeared.
Wait half a century
blessed
the patience of pain,
vastness of helplessness,
abyss of silence
-        and allowed to pray aloud...

Translation: MBS

Photo No. 20. Germans discover death pits in Katyń; 1943.

MY FATHER: A PORTRAIT FROM IMAGINATION

by Witomiła Wołk-Jezierska

A portrait from my imagination is the only one I can have, since my father was brutally murdered by the Soviets in the Katyń forest when I was only three-months old. All that remained was my ability to imagine his self, his personality, meaning—all of those things that characterize a father and allow one to feel his presence, love, care and help.

I was robbed of this experience in a most brutal manner. The image of a family with happy parents—including my mother's smile toward my father and their smiles toward me—were stolen from me. The only thing that remains are the words that I utter only in my thoughts: "father and daddy."

Photo No: 21

A train stands at a station. In the heat of the summer, we were sitting on our bags among the members of military families returning to Poland from Romania. A soldier in a *rubashka*[1] stretched out his hand towards me with half of a watermelon and said to my mother "please let her have it. I have a daughter like her back home and I am returning to Russia to her from the front."

He was returning from the war just like my Daddy. We are *en route* to see him. Now I am sure that in Poland we will meet my Father. I did not know Poland for I was born abroad, but my Grandfather says that Poland is my Fatherland. Maybe we will have to wait a little bit since the trains were chugging along slowly and Poland was so far away, but it doesn't matter. I'll wait.

---

1 Russian-type peasant shirt.

Finally, on one autumn day, a man in a soldier's coat knocked on our door. My heart leaped with joy. Daddy! It must be Daddy! Soon he will embrace my skinny shoulders with his powerful arms, he will raise me up, rub his coarse cheeks up against my face, and he will wonder how big I have become. After all, he has never seen me before.

I became engulfed by a powerful wave of joy, and I awaited something which—in spite of the love of my mother and grandparents—I had never known but was sure was beautiful.

Suddenly my mother called out to me: "Your uncle just arrived from the German POW camp, come greet him!" The great beautiful dream suddenly crumbled and the awakening was terrible. All who were to return have already returned.

Bang! Bang! Bang! I listened to their conversation by the door. First there was the radio signal, and then news about the Katyń Forest, about Polish officers, and about the greatest massacre in the world that was committed on the Polish military there.

This was the time when I already knew that my father was killed and buried there. But in spite of this—contrary to the facts—I trusted that he was still alive. I awaited the fulfillment of my dreams of his return. This wait for something that could not possibly occur leaves such a painful lump in the throat.

****

In the city park there is a single grave with a red star instead of a cross. The soldier was buried where he died, in a typical wartime grave. As I pass by it, I think about my father's grave and its location; after all, anyone killed during the war has a grave. What happened to my father, the Polish officer? I don't know how he and his companions were buried.

My Grandpa—who was a Major of the "Sanacja Army," as the communists called the Polish Army,[2]—never taught me to hate, even after he was released from a communist secret police prison as a handicap. He was a great patriot, hence "a reactionary and an enemy of the Soviet system." He differentiated good from evil, the murdered from the murderers, and the victims from the executioners, even if they were of the same ethnicity.

Grandpa shared a common personality with his son-in-law, that is my father, and taught me the same values. I saw how his daughters respected him. He was an example to me, as respect and love for my father formed in my conscience; the father whose image emerged from family stories and recollections of friends in the imagination of a child, a girl, and a woman.

Family stories about my father are often specific. Usually they are recollections of some events, a few warm thoughts, and grief that everything was so short-lived. The remainder of their recollections became an internal dialogue, as if he, my Father, stood right there with them. Heads were full of thought. The images that came before their eyes were only meant for them. They were smiling, as if

2 The Sanacja was the political block of Józef Piłsudski and his successors who ruled Poland in the interwar period.

the smiles were meant for him. This experience showed how close they were with my Dad and how difficult it was to speak about him when they imagined him. The silence that ensued was just like the stillness following the death or some other tragedy which befell someone. The sadness is all the greater the greater that person was.

*****

The young secondary school student on the photograph is so handsome that no one can rival him. My mom laughed: "This was your father when he attended the Father Piramowicz Secondary School in Cisna." I looked through all of my father's pictures. I enlarged the pictures of street scenes to draw a portrait of my father in my imagination. He seemed almost always serious and full of thought. His eyes were blue and his hair light.

Just as one glues together a disintegrated archeological find to discern its shape by following descriptions from books or stories, so I too attempted to create an image of my father in my mind and to answer the question why my mother, a very attractive and intelligent woman after all, never again remarried and remained a widow. How great my father had to be that no one could match him. How much good that lasted a lifetime she must have experienced with him.

He also must have been a great son to his mother, who took two of his diplomas form school on her deportation journey to Soviet Kazakhstan and then the exodus through Persia to England. The diplomas show that my father graduated from Volhynian M. Kątski Artillery Reserve Officers' School in Włodzimierz Wołyński and the Artillery School for Officer Cadre in Toruń. He was first assigned to X Artillery Regiment in Przemyśl. In March 1938 he was promoted to lieutenant, received permission to get married from the military authorities, and married my mother.

On August 12, 1938, Dad was appointed as an instructor at the J. Bem Artillery Reserve Officer School in Zambrów. He wanted to teach at the Military Academy, but fate brought other designs for him.

"Wait for me, I shall return soon," he wrote in a postcard from the Kozielsk prisoner-of-war camp in the Soviet Union. "I come for your baptism in a free Poland." His small and legible handwriting filled the entire page. There was news about his brothers-in-arms, joy from the news about my birth, best wishes, longing, and so many dreams for a future together. All he wanted to do was to return! He was very much needed; he knew that he was needed, and he wanted to be with us forever.

What my father wrote provides the best possible profile of him. This postcard tells me everything about him. Thus, I know that he was a gentle, good, responsible, and loving man. Each sentence he penned was full of love and care for his family, wife, child, in-laws, and Poland. He trusted that our country will be liberated. In spite of the tragic conditions in the POW camp, he never complained but thought only about his family and our time together in the future.

Everyone who knew my father testified to the strength of his character.

As far back as I can remember, an icon of the Virgin Mary of Kozielsk has been hanging over my mother's bed. I experience so many thoughts and emotions about my mother and father when this painting comes to my mind. This Kozielsk icon has been intimately connected with the Katyń victims even though it was painted after the Katyń massacre.

To this day my father's uniform coat hangs in our closet. It is beautiful and well-maintained. As I touch the cloth, I imagine how I would feel in my father's arms. When I look at my daughter as her father throws her up in the air, I always think how much I would give for one such moment with my father.

A depiction of a victim whose uniform was torn off compelled my mother to ask: "What is this, my God, who is this? How can this be? Why is this not a military man?" And then my mother began to tell me about how much a uniform meant to my father and his fellow officers, how proud they were of it, and how much they cared for it. She then reminded me of the uniform coat hanging in the closet.

A great difference may exist between our reading of the list of massacred Polish officers and the interpretation of other people. We will always see them as soldiers of the Polish Army.

Finally, we forced ourselves to cross the fate and read the tiny obituary in the *Nowy Kurier Warszawski* dated June 27, 1943: "02564, Wołk, Wincenty, Lt., Found: 3 military decorations, a letter, and a postcard."

Much later came the time to touch the soil which took him in, and to see his last destination, Gnezdovo station, and to ponder this genocide and the loneliness he must have felt in the clutches of his Soviet oppressors over the execution pit.

What a crude prelude to the massacre must have been the ride in the cattle car and the "Black Raven" van. His last meal was a salted herring—which must have been worse than a sponge filled with bile and vinegar—to wear him down through thirst. The death must have been horrific, macabre and unimaginable. And there was also the exhaustion, hopelessness, fear, and despair. Was all of this sufficient to qualify it as martyrdom?

When I look through the Diary of Daily School Orders, I have counted more than sixty of my father's friends, all murdered, including two commandants of the Officers' School, Colonels Jasiński and Chylewski, the commander of X Artillery Regiment, Col. Bokszczanin, and countless others well known to my grandfather and our family.

I know that they perished because they fought for the independence of Poland, for Poland's rebirth in 1918 after 123 years of partitions, for the victory over the Bolsheviks in 1920 war, for patriotism, democracy, and so many other things that the Soviet regime could not grant them, and for being the "intransigent enemies of the Soviet regime." They were sentenced not only to die, but also to be forgotten, and to have their names, and the name of the Polish Army whose cadre they formed, slandered. The only hope is that we will never forget!

Photo No. 24. Artillery Reserve Mazovia Cadet School of Gen. Józef Bem in Zambrów.

In the church of the Holiest Trinity in Zambrów Witomiła Wołk-Jezierska initiated the installation of a plaque honoring the martyr deaths of 72 officers, instructors at the Mazovian Artillery Reserve Officers' School and the Volhynian M. Kątski School in Włodzimierz Wołyński. These officers, including her father, were captured by the Soviets on September 20, 1939 in Włodzimierz Wołyński, held as prisoners-of-war for half a year, then brutally murdered in the spring of 1940 in Katyń and Kharkov.

THE FAMILY DEFINED BY KATYŃ

by Witomiła Wołk-Jezierska

I am a daughter of Lieutenant Wincenty Witold Wołk who was a lecturer at the Mazovia School of Artillery in Zambrów. My mother, Ojcumiła nee Gancarz, was a daughter of Ferdinand Gancarz, doctor who served as Major in the Artillery Regiment of the Polish Army in Przemyśl. My parents were married in 1938, and at the end of August 1939 they parted forever.

In September 1939, when Germans and Soviets invaded Poland, my grandfather operated a veterinary hospital in Przemyśl, in south-eastern Poland. On September 17, 1939, when the Red Army entered Poland, he was on his way from Przemyśl towards the south-eastern border. He found himself in Kołomyja and realized that he would not be able to join my father who was then in Włodzimierz Wołyński. So, my grandfather and my mother decided to cross the border via Kuty to Romania. They safely made it to Romania and several months later, in January of 1940, I was born there.

As soon as my father learned about the military draft, he sent my mother who was pregnant to her family to Przemyśl. On September 6, 1939 the Mazovia School was evacuated from Zambrów to Włodzimierz Wołyński where the Wołyń Officer Cadet School was located. There, in the night from 19 to 20 of September 1939, they were taken as prisoners of war by the Red Army. Subsequently, my father was transferred to the Kozielsk prisoner-of-war camp and on April 30, 1940 was murdered in Katyń.

At one point, the prisoners of war in the Kozielsk camps were allowed to write one letter per month to the families. Of course they all searched for their families. So did my father. We assume that most likely my father wrote to his mother who lived in Lóżki with her family, it's near Cisna, northern Poland. For sure he also wrote to Przemyśl, and we don't know from where, most likely from Przemyśl, he received my mother and grandfather's address in Romania. The letter from my father was not the first one because in the meantime my mother found his address in Kozielsk and wrote to him that I was born. I can't tell how my mother obtained my father's address in Kozielsk but soon after my birth on January 22, 1940, she wrote to my father, probably in early February 1940, that I was born and how I was named. To her letter my father replied with a postcard - in fact at the very last moment - just weeks before he was murdered.

So, we knew that my father learned about my birth but after that - our contact ended abruptly …

My name "Witomiła" is a combination of my father's name, because he was called Witek, and my mother's shortened name Miła. That is how the name Witomiła came about and this name made my father very happy.

At the very last moment, my father was able to send us a postcard from Kozielsk to Romania, to the address of my grandfather. This postcard is dated April 10, 1940. Shortly after that date, an order was issued prohibiting any correspondence for the Kozielsk POWs, whether outgoing or coming into the camp. In this postcard my father wrote that he and his colleagues around are very happy about my birth. He also wrote that they would return to free Poland for my baptism, and we were very much looking into it.

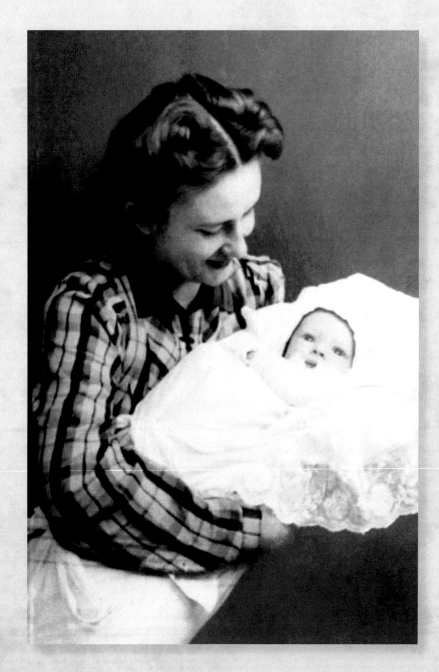

Photo No. 26. Ojcumiła Wotk with Daughter Witomiła, Romania 1940.

My father was also making plans about my name together with his colleagues. He wrote to my mother that they came up with a name Bożena for me but that he was very happy that I was given the name Witomiła.

My mother waited a long time with my baptism. In fact, I was baptized when I returned to Poland as a 5-year-old girl. I have 3 names: Witomiła, Maria Bożena. I was baptized in the Przemyśl Cathedral and I remember very well my baptism because I responded to all the questions myself. Several years ago, I went back to Przemyśl and visited Archbishop Michalik there. He showed me where the baptismal bowl stood. We talked about my baptism, this strangely sad event.

The consequences of my father searching for us from the POW camp were severe. He did not know that we ended up in Romania. So he kept writing to his mother to Lóżki near Cisna. He also wrote to my family in Przemyśl. As it turned out, only just now we learn that the consequence of such inquiries were deadly, resulting in the deportation of the entire family of my father, his mother and sister with children, from this place Lóżki near Cisna. It is interesting that only one sister of my father avoided deportation because when the NKVD came for them she was not in Lóżki. She was called with a horse cart somewhere.

Also many members of my mother's family in Przemyśl were deported to USSR. Przemyśl was split between German and Soviet occupation. So all those under the Soviet occupation were deported as well. They ended up either in Kazakstan or near the North Pole. I think they were deported on April 13, 1940. This date indicates that they were deported as part of the Katyń operation – for sure.

I don't even know the name of the place to which my grandmother, my father's mother with her family was deported. However, they all left this Soviet inhumane land with the Anders Army, but never returned to Poland. After the war, they all settled in England or left for Canada. This applies to both sides of my family, those from my father side and those from my mother side, all those who found themselves in eastern Poland occupied by the Soviet Union.

My grandfather, who was a Major in the Polish Army, crossed the Polish-Romanian border based on some agreement between Poland and Romania singed many years earlier. Romania guaranteed camps for interned Polish officers. As a veterinary doctor, my grandfather did not have to stay in the camp, but had to report on a regular basis. The internment camp was mandatory for all active officers.

The internment camps were located in attractive locations in the facilities not used during the war by the Romanians. These were Trigoviszte, Baylegovoraj, these types of small places. From what I understand from my aunt who was also together with us, and from recollections of my grandfather, the top officials of the Government of Poland were held in these internment camps.

We stayed in Romania to the end of the war. Once during the war my family attempted to return to Poland but was stopped at the border. My grandfather brought me back to Poland on August 15, 1945, together with my mother and my aunt, my mother's sister. We crossed the border in Sanok, and traveled to Przemyśl, because before the war the entire family had lived in Przemyśl for centuries.

My Godfather offered us an apartment in Przemyśl. We stayed there but my grandfather did not want to serve in the army of communist Poland. So he left Przemyśl in search for a civilian job as a veterinary doctor. We moved with him and settled in Warmia.

*****

My father was always on our minds. Ever since the 1940 postcard from Kozielsk - his last correspondence - there were no further letters. My grandfather diligently followed all the news regarding this matter. In 1943, around June I think, the name of my father appeared on the lists of the Katyń victims in some Polish newspapers.

My grandfather learned about the identification of my father in Katyń but he did not tell my mother about it. She learned about the death of my father only after returning to Poland, from some family papers, letters. She went through this trauma only after the war.

And I was waiting because the assumption of such small children who played together in Romania, and there was several of us there, we trusted that we go to Poland and wait for our fathers there. So, I had been still waiting for my father.

Upon return to Poland, when we were in Warmia, one evening a bell rang. As a curious youngster watching from the staircase, I noticed that an officer came to the house. He was dressed in the overcoat with a military cap. So, obviously it had to be my father, right? This dreamed about father of mine!

No! It turned out that this was a brother of my grandfather who survived the entire war in the German POW camp and came to his brother to say hello. That is how my waiting for the father ended because it occurred to me that besides this new granduncle no one else would show up anymore.

I don't recall whether someone would say to me directly that my father was killed in Katyń. My grandfather often listened to London broadcast and I remember very well how I would listen from behind the door. Those characteristic sounds like bum, bum, something like that. One day there was a long program about Katyń, about the Katyń forest. And this caused in me a great fear. For a young child, a forest is connected with something secretive, bad. The grandfather never told me about it. It was… I can't explain it… But all of this consisted of some vague hints. In school Katyń was never discussed.

Probably it had to be said at some point directly by my grandfather. He told me once that I was forbidden to ever deal with any political matters, that it is my sole duty to study and become someone in life. These were the directives of my grandfather.

Long after my graduation from high school, I learned that my grandfather had told my history teacher in strict confidence that my father was killed in Katyń. However, I think that everybody in that town knew that my father was killed in Katyń. One day a man showed up. He came from my father's town and kept blackmailing my mother. She had difficulties to keep her job because that man was above her. These were the types of harassments and threats that she has been experiencing all the time.

The principals of my high school were high ranking members of the Communist Party. They most likely did not know. I think the school did not know.

When did I realize? Not necessarily realized but rather felt the lack of the father. I felt this loss the most acutely after the death of my grandfather in 1972. He was an exceptional man, a great intellectual, wrote beautiful poetry, was interested and knew Greek in addition to Latin, was fluent in German. Only after his death, when it became possible to talk openly about Katyń, I got involved in this matter.

*****

For a long time, I had been unable to force myself to read the Katyń lists. I don't remember the year, but I was already an adult when I did it. It was after my graduation from the university. Working as a conservator, I once asked for these newspapers from 1943 and I simply searched for the name of my father. I found him under the June date, about June 27, in the newspaper. It was, it was like an obituary of my father...

I went to Katyń for the first time on April 5, 1989. This was the greatest shock I ever experienced in my life. That is when I wrote poems dedicated to my Father. Since that moment, I began to immerse myself in the question of his last journey from Zambrów to Katyń. I wrote a book *Untold Story of the Katyń Crime* and several articles.

Analyzing all available documentation, analyzing Memoir of Prof. Świaniewicz, I finally discovered the day on which my father was murdered. It was on April 30, 1940. Świaniewicz describes very well this day, a beautiful April morning, sunny, with birds singing, while they were led to their death in Katyń…

Since that time I must say, I strive to make sure that justice is served for this crime. The result of this commitment is my efforts to sue Russia in the European Tribunal for Human Rights in Strasbourg. However, my most important goal that I have to achieve is to make sure that the remains of my father return home! I know exactly where, in which place, in which row, in which layer, he is buried in Katyń. He must return home to Poland at last!

Photo No. 27. Polish Officers; Project by Stanisław Drabczyński.

The order to murder all Polish officers held as POWs in the Soviet Union signed by Joseph Stalin on March 5, 1940 was executed in blatant violation of the Geneva Convention and all international customary laws and civilized norms. The Katyn genocide carefully covered up, eliminated from consideration at the Nuremberg trials, and erased from memory of World War Two, was never recognized as a high crime by the international community. The Stalinist leaders who ordered the murders and the NKVD executioners who carried out the killings were never prosecuted for their crimes, and the victims were never properly honored, buried and rehabilitated. The moral calculus with respect to this crime of all crimes has not been worked out to this day.

Photo No. 28. Katyń Monument in Niles / Chicago, USA; April 10, 2010.

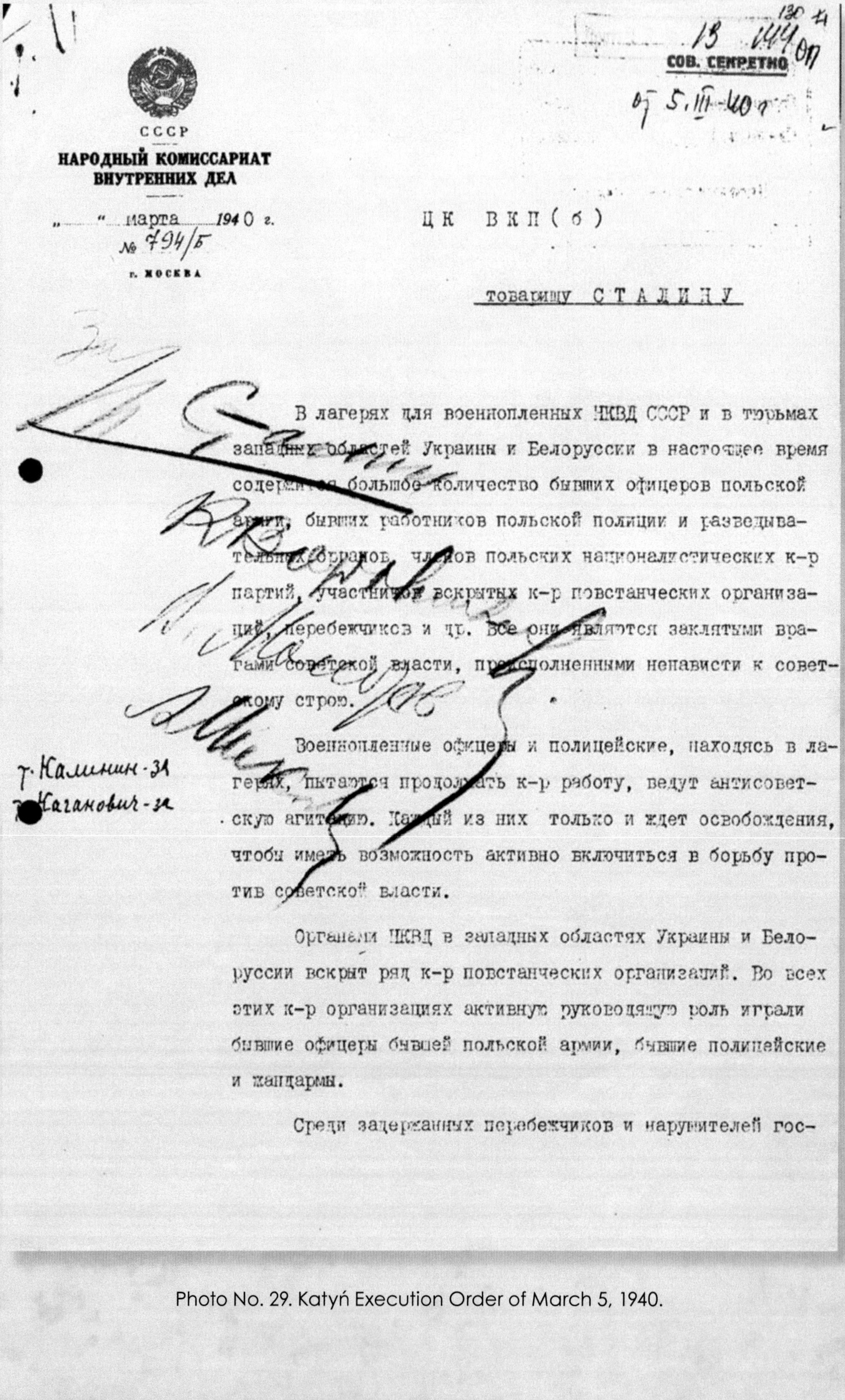

СССР

**НАРОДНЫЙ КОМИССАРИАТ
ВНУТРЕННИХ ДЕЛ**

"___" марта 1940 г.
№ 794/Б

г. МОСКВА

СОВ. СЕКРЕТНО

ЦК ВКП(б)

товарищу СТАЛИНУ

В лагерях для военнопленных НКВД СССР и в тюрьмах западных областей Украины и Белоруссии в настоящее время содержится большое количество бывших офицеров польской армии, бывших работников польской полиции и разведывательных органов, членов польских националистических к-р партий, участников вскрытых к-р повстанческих организаций, перебежчиков и пр. Все они являются заклятыми врагами советской власти, преисполненными ненависти к советскому строю.

Военнопленные офицеры и полицейские, находясь в лагерях, пытаются продолжать к-р работу, ведут антисоветскую агитацию. Каждый из них только и ждет освобождения, чтобы иметь возможность активно включиться в борьбу против советской власти.

Органами НКВД в западных областях Украины и Белоруссии вскрыт ряд к-р повстанческих организаций. Во всех этих к-р организациях активную руководящую роль играли бывшие офицеры бывшей польской армии, бывшие полицейские и жандармы.

Среди задержанных перебежчиков и нарушителей гос-

т. Калинин - за
Каганович - за

Photo No. 29. Katyń Execution Order of March 5, 1940.

KATYŃ EXECUTION ORDER
MARCH 5, 1940, USSR POLITBIURO

The prisoner-of-war camps are holding a total of **14,736** detainees who are more than **97% POLISH BY NATIONALITY.**

In the prisons of western oblasts of Ukraine and Belorussia a total of **18,632** arrested people, including **10,685 Poles,** are held.

Based on the fact that they are all hardened irremediable enemies of Soviet power, the NKVD USSR believes it is essential to examine the cases of:

a) 14,700 former Polish officers

b) 11,000 of those arrested who are in the prisons in western oblasts of Ukraine and Belorussia, and apply to them the supreme punishment [execution] by shooting.

TO BE KILLED by SHOOTING:

- **14,700** Polish officers held as prisoner of war
- **11,000** Polish civilian citizens detained in conquered Poland

TOTAL: 25,700 CARRIERS OF POLISH IDENTITY

Photo No. 30. Jam Saheb with Polish Children from Deportees Camp in Balachadi, India, 1944.

Photo No. 31. Reunion of Polish deportees from Balachadi Camp; Orchard Lake, USA, 2013.

USSR POLITBIURO ON DEPORTATIONS MARCH 2, 1940

Top Secret

Special Folder

Approve the following proposals by Comrades Beria and Khrushchev:

2. Direct the USSR MKVD to do the following:

a) by April 15 of this year deport to the district of the Kazakh SSR for a term of ten years all the families of the repressed and those who are now in prisoner-of-war camps, former officers of the Polish Army, police, prison guards, gendarmes, intelligence agents, former landowners, manufacturers, and prominent officials in the former Polish state apparatus, numbering 22,000 to 25,000 families.

Excerpts from Protocol no. 13, Decisions of the Politburo on Guarding the State borders of the Ukrainian SSR and Byelorussian SSR, pursuant to which families of the Katyń victims in the Soviet-occupied part of Poland were deported to Kazakhstan in April 1940.

Photo No. 32

Photo No. 33

SHELAPIN'S MEMO

Chairman, the Committee for State Security, USSR Council of Ministers, A. Shelapin Memo to Krushchev dated March 3, 1959 Proposing to Destroy the Documents of the Operation Sanctioned by the Politburo on March 5, 1940. This memo reveals that at least 21,857 Polish citizens were murdered pursuant to the Katyń Execution Order.

Polish Officers POWs:

4,421 Katyń (Kozielsk POW Camp, Smolensk Oblast)

3,821 Piatichatki (Starobielsk Camp near Kharkov)

6,311 Miednoje (Ostaszkow Camp, Kalinin Oblast)

Polish Civilians:

7,305 (Kuropaty, Bykownia, Kherzon, Odessa, Niezyn &...)

21,857 TOTAL

Even up to additional **800 mass burial sites** of the Polish nationals murdered by the Soviets could be still found on the territory of the former Soviet Union according to the "Memorial" Human Rights Group in Russia.

Photo No. 34. The Katyń Pantheon; Project by StanisławDrabczyński.

Union Calendar No. 792

THE KATYN FOREST MASSACRE

FINAL REPORT

OF THE

SELECT COMMITTEE TO CONDUCT AN INVESTIGATION AND STUDY OF THE FACTS, EVIDENCE, AND CIRCUMSTANCES OF THE KATYN FOREST MASSACRE

PURSUANT TO

H. Res. 390

AND

H. Res. 539

(82d Congress)

A RESOLUTION TO AUTHORIZE THE INVESTIGATION OF THE MASS MURDER OF POLISH OFFICERS IN THE KATYN FOREST NEAR SMOLENSK, RUSSIA

FROM
RAY J. MADDEN
Congressman
FIRST DISTRICT - INDIANA

DECEMBER 22, 1952.—Committed to the Committee of the Whole House on the State of the Union and ordered to be printed

---

UNITED STATES
GOVERNMENT PRINTING OFFICE
26668
WASHINGTON : 1952

MADDEN COMMITTEE
FINAL REPORT, DECEMBER 22, 1952

Select Committee to Conduct an Investigation and Study of the Facts, Evidence and Circumstances of the Katyń Forest Massacre - US Congress Report No. 2505

Excerpts from Conclusions

This committee has come to the conclusion that in those fateful days nearing the end of the Second World War there unfortunately existed in high government and military circles strange psychosis that military necessity required the sacrifice of loyal allies and our own principles in order to keep Soviet Russia from making a separate piece with the Nazis (Germany).

This psychosis continued even after the conclusion of the war.

This committee believes that had the Van Vliet report been made immediately available to the Department of State and to the American public, the course of our government policy towards Soviet Russia might have been more realistic with more fortunate post-war results.

Through the disastrous failure to recognize the danger sign which then existed and in following a policy of satisfying the Kremlin leaders, our Government unwittingly strengthened their hand and contributed to a situation which has grown to be a menace to the United State and the entire free world.

The program of silencing Polish radio commentators went beyond the scope of their duties as official Government representatives.

This committee noted the striking similarity between crimes committed against the Poles at Katyń and those being inflicted on American and other United Nation troops in Korea.

Photo No. 35.
American POWs
at Katyń, May 1943.

LIST OF PHOTOGRAPHS

1. Cover Photo: Libra Institute, Inc.
2. Witomiła Wołk-Jezierska, Photo: Tomasz Parol, forumemjot.wordpress.com, 2014
3. Jersey City Katyń Monument in the Atelier of Master A. Pityński.
4. Winceny Wołk, Officer of the Polish Army; Photo: Witomiła Wołk-Jezierska (W.W.J)
5. A Button, Narodowe Centrum Kultury; Gość niedzielny.
6. Winceny Wołk and Ojcumiła Gancarz Wołk; Photo: W.W.J.
7. Kozielsk Postcard of April 10, 1940 from W. Wołk to M. Gancarowa; Photo: W.W.J.
8. The Dead Forest; Photo: Libra Institute, Inc.
9. The Katyń Monument in Jersey City against the backdrop of WTC. Photo: A. Pityński
10. The Katyń Monument in Jersey City, September 11, 2001; Photo: A. Pityński.
11. Tied Hands of the Katyń Victim, Katyń Museum, Warsaw, Poland.
12. Nine Eleven Commemoration Plaque at the Plinth of Katyń Monument in Jersey City.
13. Husar by A. Pityński, Polish Cemetery in Doylestown, Pennsylvania. Photo: G. Tymiński.
14. Farewell, Painting by Marek Jeliński, Photo: W.W. J.
15. Flower. Photo: httpspixabay.com
16. Katyń Families at the Katyń Memorial, Gunnersbury, UK, 1976. Photo: Czesław Siegieda.
17. Relics from the Katyń graves, Photo 1943, Katyń Museum.
18. April 5, 1989 Commemorative Mass and Taking of Soil in the Katyń Forest. Photo: W.W.J.
19. Katyń Monument by A. Pityński, Baltimore, Maryland.
20. German Army advancing east discovers death pits in Katyń; Photo: 1943 Katyń Museum.
21. A Cap of the Polish Army Soldier; Photo: Katyń Museum.
22. Fragment of the Katyń Monument in Jersey City, New Jersey. Photo: G. Tymiński.
23. Saint Mary of Kozielsk; Photo: W.W. J.
24. Artillery Reserve Mazovia Cadet School of Gen. Józef Bem in Zambrów; Photo: W.W. J.
25. Witomiła Wołk-Jezierska; Photo: Libra Institute, Inc.
26. Ojcumiła Wołk with Daughter Witomiła, Romania 1940. Photo: W.W. J.
27. National Katyń Pantheon, Stanisław Drabczyński Project; www.pomnikofiarKatyńia.pl
28. Katyń Monument in Niles / Chicago, Illinois, USA. Photo: M. Mucha, en.wikipedia.org.
29. Katyń Execution Order, Photo: Russian archive RGASPI, wikipedia.org, Libra Institute, Inc.
30. Jam Saheb with Polish Children from Balachadi Camp in Jamnagar; CSPA, Culture.pl.
31. Reunion of Polish Deportees from Balachadi Camp; Orchard Lake, Michigan, USA, 2013.
32. Exhumed bodies in Katyń Forest; Zbrodnia Katyńska w Świetle Dokumentów, 1946.
33. Photographs of Polish Officers Murdered in Katyń, Katyń Museum.
34. National Katyń Pantheon; S. Drabczyński Project. www.pomnikofiarKatyńia.pl.
35. American POW John H. Van Vliet and Donald B. Stewart in Katyń, May 1943; pl.wikipedia.
36. Back Cover: Katyń Monument in Jersey City, September 11, 2001; Photo: A. Pityński.